INTRODUCTION

Whether you are sorting laundry in the bedroom or organizing yo[ur] workbench in the garage, you can turn your house into a teaching house just by using ordinary items in ordinary rooms in any type of home.

Teaching House is divided into five chapters: Living-Dining Room, Kitchen, Bedroom, Bathroom, and Garage. Within each chapter there are fun, easy ideas for activities in such areas as language, creativity, thinking skills, coordination, science, and self-awareness.

At first glance, these activities might seem to be "just play." However, as the introductory sentences to the activities explain, each utilizes a specific skill—one that forms part of a foundation necessary for higher learning.

For instance, participating in dramatic-play and oral-language activities prepares your child for communicating clearly with others. Art projects spark the imagination needed for effective reading, writing, and scientific speculation. Playing matching and sorting games develops an understanding of likes and differences, a skill used in nearly all learning areas, including math, science, reading, and writing. Small-muscle coordination activities pave the way for learning how to use a pen or pencil; science activities promote thinking skills; and self-esteem activities lead to developing self-confidence, so necessary for your child's success in all learning areas.

If the rooms of your home differ from our labels, just adapt the activities to fit a different area. For instance, most of the Bedroom activities could easily be done in the Living-Dining Room, and many of the Garage projects on a porch or deck.

Since you are your child's first teacher, take this opportunity to start teaching him or her basic skills and concepts right now. Just open to a page for the room you are in, skim through the easy step-by-step instructions, and begin!

A WORD ABOUT SAFETY

Keep in mind that when doing the activities, an adult should supervise to make sure that children do not place materials or objects in their mouths. As for art materials, such as scissors, glue, or felt tip markers, use those that are specifically labeled as safe for children unless the materials are to be used only by an adult.

CONTENTS

LIVING-DINING ROOM

PHOTO STORIES

Family photos provide rich details for this oral-language activity.

1) Collect a number of family photographs, including pictures of yourself when you were young.

2) Invite your child to sit with you.

3) As you look through the photos, help your child name each of the people pictured.

4) Ask your child to tell what is happening in each photograph.

ANOTHER IDEA: Glue photos of your family members on separate index cards. Print names under the photos and staple the cards together to make a book for your child to "read."

OBJECT SOUNDS

This game helps develop listening skills using familiar objects.

1) Set out three or four familiar objects that make different sounds when tapped, such as a book, a framed photo, a cup, and a spoon.

2) Give your child time to examine the objects.

3) Ask your child to close his or her eyes while you tap one of the objects with a pencil.

4) Have your child try to guess, by its sound, which object you are tapping.

5) Let your child open his or her eyes to see if the guess was close.

6) Follow the same procedure with the other objects. Or, let your child have a turn being the tapper.

AGE VARIATION: For older children, make the game more challenging by tapping objects at random around the room.

TREASURE HUNT

This activity promotes listening skills using an audio tape and a tape recorder.

1) Select a "treasure" such as stickers, paper cutouts, or new crayons.

2) Hide the treasure in the room in a place where your child can easily reach it.

3) Tape-record directions for finding the treasure.

4) Let your child search for the treasure while listening to the tape and following the clues.

LETTER SEARCH

Your child will enjoy "reading the newspaper" with this letter-recognition activity.

1) Give your child a page from a newspaper and a felt tip marker.

2) Print the first letter of your child's name, to serve as a guide, on a piece of note paper.

3) Ask your child to search through the newspaper page to find that letter.

4) Whenever your child discovers the letter, have him or her circle it with the marker.

5) Continue in the same manner with other alphabet letters, having your child use markers of different colors to circle them.

WHAT'S INSIDE?

Gift-wrapping a familiar object makes this predicting activity especially fun.

1) Use tissue paper and tape to wrap a familiar object.

2) Show the package to your child and ask him or her to guess what's inside.

3) Give as many clues as necessary. For instance, if you wrapped a toy car, you might say: "You play with it. It is red. It has four wheels. It rolls on the floor."

4) When your child guesses correctly, let him or her open the package.

5) Invite your child to wrap an object and have you guess what it is.

BOOK LINE-UP

Let your child help you organize a bookshelf with this ordering activity.

1) Clear a shelf of a low bookcase.

2) Place books of various heights in a pile next to the bookcase.

3) Have your child arrange the books on the shelf from tallest to shortest or from shortest to tallest.

MEASURING WITH YARN

This math activity will help your child begin to learn about measurements.

1) Cut a piece of yarn about 12 inches long.

2) Let your child use the yarn piece to "measure" the lengths, widths, or heights of furniture pieces such as tables or chairs.

3) Ask questions such as these: "How many yarn pieces high is the table? How many yarn pieces long is the rug?"

ANOTHER IDEA: Cut pieces of yarn the exact width (or other dimension) of objects in the room, such as a table, a bookcase, and a TV set. Help your child discover which pieces fit which objects.

ALIKE AND DIFFERENT

Classification activities like this one help your child develop thinking skills.

1) On a table, place five or six common objects, such as a key, a pencil, a book, a box, and a rubber ball.

2) Ask your child to notice the sizes, shapes, materials, and colors of the objects.

3) Have your child tell you how the objects are alike and how they are different.

AGE VARIATION: For younger children, ask direct questions such as: "Which objects are the same color? Which object is a toy? Which objects are not toys?"

GIFT-WRAP BOARD GAME

Reusing gift wrap is fun with this easy-to-make matching game.

1) Select a piece of gift-wrap that contains a pattern of small pictures.

2) Cut out a large square of the paper and tape it to a piece of cardboard to make a gameboard.

3) From an identical square of the gift-wrap, cut out the small pictures to make game pieces.

4) Let your child play the game by placing the game pieces on top of the matching pictures on the gameboard.

HINT: To make the game more durable, cover the gameboard and the game pieces on both sides with clear self-stick paper. Attach an envelope to the back of the board to hold the game pieces.

SHAPE SEARCH

Use this shape-recognition activity to make your child aware of the geometric shapes all around us.

1) Draw a rectangle on a piece of paper.

2) Show the rectangle to your child and talk about its shape.

3) Ask your child to look around the room to find other rectangles: chair backs, pictures on the wall, windows, doors, and so forth.

4) Follow the same procedure to help your child discover circles, squares, and triangles in the room.

POSTCARD PUZZLES

Working with jigsaw puzzles is a great problem-solving activity that also involves coordination skills.

1) Collect several used or new postcards.

2) Cut each postcard into three to six interlocking puzzle pieces, depending on the age and ability of your child.

3) Store the pieces of each puzzle in a separate envelope.

4) Give the puzzles to your child and let him or her put the pieces together.

HINT: To make the puzzles more durable, mount the postcards on heavy paper and cover them on both sides with clear self-stick paper before cutting them into pieces.

WINDOW WASHER

Letting your child help wash windows is a great way to promote large-muscle development.

1) Clear the area around a glass door or large window and cover the floor with newspaper.

2) Give your child glass cleaner, made by mixing 2 quarts water with 2 tablespoons lemon juice, and some paper towels.

3) Show your child how to apply the cleaner to the glass and wipe with the paper towels.

4) Encourage your child to move his or her arms up and down and back and forth in large, sweeping movements.

5) To finish the job, let your child crumple clean sheets of newspaper and use them to polish the glass.

FEELINGS BOOK

This self-esteem activity provides opportunities for your child to explore different feelings.

1) Select five pieces of paper for book pages.

2) Using a pen, label the pages with these words: "Happy," "Sad," "Mad," "Scared," and "Excited."

3) With your child, look through old magazines to find pictures of people whose expressions look like these feelings.

4) Help your child cut or tear out the pictures and glue them onto the appropriate pages.

5) Staple the pages together with a plain paper cover to make a book. Print "Feelings Book" on the front.

6) As your child "reads" the book to you, discuss different feelings and how it is okay to have them.

PINHOLE MAGNIFIER

Your child will use observation skills with this science activity.

1) Select a small index card.

2) Use a pin to make a hole in the center of the card.

3) Wiggle the pin around until the hole is just large enough to see through.

4) Give the card to your child and let him or her walk around the room, looking at various objects through the hole in the card.

5) Ask your child to tell you how the objects look different. (They look larger. When an object is viewed through the magnifier, the usual cues from other objects are blocked, making it difficult to judge size.)

MOVABLE CHAIRS

Your child is sure to imagine great adventures with this dramatic-play activity.

1) Move the chairs from around your dining room table into a cleared space in the room.

2) Let your child rearrange the chairs to create a make-believe scene such as the inside of a car.

3) Encourage your child to sit in the car and go for a pretend ride, taking dolls or stuffed animals along as passengers.

4) Have your child describe where the car is going and what he or she sees along the way.

5) Suggest other make-believe scenes for your child to create with the chairs, such as the inside of a bus, an airplane, a theater, or a school.

LET'S PLAY CARDS

Ordinary playing cards are great to use for sorting activities like these.

1) Remove the face cards from a deck of ordinary playing cards.

2) Use the remaining cards for games such as those that follow.

- Show your child how to sort the cards by color, placing all the red cards in one pile and all the black cards in another pile.

- Have your child sort the cards by suit, placing all the clubs in one pile, the spades in a second pile, the hearts in a third pile, and the diamonds in a fourth pile.

- Let your child sort the cards by number, placing all the 2s in one pile, the 3s in a second pile, the 4s in a third pile, and so forth.

ANOTHER IDEA: For a different kind of learning game, have your child line up the cards in patterns, such as red-black-red-black or heart-club-diamond-heart-club-diamond.

COIN RUBBINGS

Help your child become more observant of textures with this art activity using coins.

1) Collect several different coins.

2) Attach the coins to a tabletop with short pieces of tape rolled sticky-side out.

3) Have your child place a piece of thin paper on top of the coins. Secure the paper with tape to keep it from moving around.

4) Show your child how to color over the coins with the sides of peeled crayons to make rubbings.

ANOTHER IDEA: Turn this activity into a learning game by having your child match the coins to the rubbings.

KITCHEN

PAPER BAG MATH

This math activity helps reinforce understanding of the meaning of numbers.

1) Select five paper lunch bags.

2) Use a pen to number the bags from 1 to 5.

3) In each numbered bag, place a corresponding number of small objects such as one paper cup, two napkins, three jar lids, and so forth.

4) Give the bags to your child to play with, encouraging him or her to take the items out of the bags, count them, and compare the numbers to those written on the bags.

ANOTHER IDEA: Empty the five bags and set them out with 15 identical objects, such as plastic spoons or drinking straws. Let your child name the number on each bag and place a corresponding number of objects into each one.

SALT WRITING

This activity develops letter recognition through sight and touch.

1) Select a dark-colored baking pan with sides.

2) Pour enough salt into the pan to cover the bottom.

3) Set out a food package with letters printed on it to use as a guide, if desired.

4) Let your child use a finger to practice drawing alphabet letters in the salt.

5) Show your child how to "erase" by gently shaking the pan back and forth.

ANOTHER IDEA: For a more permanent game, use a thin, sturdy box with a lid and cover the bottom of the box with dark paper before adding the salt. Your child can use the box for drawing shapes, numbers, pictures, and so forth.

KITCHEN BOOK

An unusual homemade book makes this prereading activity lots of fun for your child.

1) Stack together three or four small resealable plastic bags with the open ends facing right.

2) Staple the bags together along the left-hand side of the stack to make a "book." Cover the staples with tape for reinforcement.

3) Cut squares out of paper to fit inside the plastic bags.

4) Cut pictures out of empty food packages and glue them on both sides of the paper squares.

5) Slip the squares into the open ends of the plastic bags.

6) Seal the bags and give the picture book to your child to "read."

HINT: Since the plastic bag "pages" of the book are resealable, you can change their contents whenever you wish.

TELEPHONE TIME

This oral-language activity is always a favorite.

1) Wash and dry two small cottage cheese or yogurt cartons to use for making a play telephone.

2) Cut a piece of string long enough to be stretched out within one room or between two rooms.

3) Use a sharp knife to poke a small hole in the bottom of one carton.

4) Thread one end of the string through the hole and knot it on the inside of the carton.

5) Follow the same procedure to attach the second carton to the other end of the string.

6) To use the play phone, talk into one carton while your child listens through the other carton, making sure that the string is always pulled taut.

HOMEMADE PLAYDOUGH

This favorite art activity promotes small-muscle development.

1) In a large bowl, let your child help mix together 1 cup all-purpose flour, 1/2 cup salt, 6 to 7 tablespoons water, and 1 tablespoon vegetable oil. Add drops of food coloring, if desired.

2) Divide the playdough into pieces and let your child play with them any way he or she wishes—rolling them into snakes, molding them into shapes, or pounding them flat with his or her fists.

3) Store the playdough in the refrigerator in an airtight container.

ANOTHER IDEA: Give your child "toys" to use with the playdough, such as foil tart pans, cookie cutters, plastic eating utensils, and kitchen gadgets. A potato masher or garlic press can be especially fun to use with playdough.

PAPER NAPKIN ART

This art activity uses food coloring to create colorful, one-of-a-kind napkins.

1) Cover the work area with newspaper.

2) Squeeze red, yellow, and blue food coloring into three separate jar lids or tart pans. Add drops of water to make the desired tint.

3) Show your child how to fold a paper napkin into fourths.

4) Let your child dip the corners and sides of the napkin into the different colors.

5) Help your child carefully unfold the napkin and lay it flat to dry.

6) Let your child repeat the process, using a new napkin each time.

ANOTHER IDEA: Give your child fluted coffee filters to fold and dip into the food coloring.

HOW MANY?

Your child is sure to have fun with this estimating activity.

1) In a resealable plastic bag, place a handful of pretzels, store coupons, or other identical small items.

2) Seal the bag, give it to your child, and ask him or her to guess how many items are inside.

3) Open the bag and count the items together to let your child check his or her estimate.

4) Place a different number of the items in the bag and have your child guess and count again.

MUFFIN TIN SORTER

This sorting activity will work with any small items you may have on hand.

1) Set out a muffin tin.

2) In a bowl, place several different kinds of dried pasta shapes, such as rigatoni, shells, and bow ties.

3) With your child, place one of each kind of pasta shape in a separate cup of the muffin tin.

4) Help your child sort the remaining pasta shapes into the appropriate muffin tin cups.

BERRY BASKET LOOM

This weaving activity helps develop small muscles using yarn and a plastic berry basket.

1) Select a plastic berry basket to use as a loom.

2) Cut a piece of string or yarn about 2 feet long.

3) Tie one end of the string or yarn to the berry basket.

4) Wrap tape around the other end of the string or yarn piece to make a "needle."

5) Give the Berry Basket Loom to your child and let him or her practice weaving the string in and out of the squares.

KITCHEN TONGS PICK-UP

This activity aids small-muscle development as well as eye-hand coordination.

1) Collect several small objects, such as a dried pasta shape, a pencil, a paper cup, and a crumpled paper napkin.

2) Place the objects in a bowl and put an empty bowl on the opposite side of the room.

3) Give your child a pair of kitchen tongs and demonstrate how to manipulate them.

4) Let your child use the tongs to remove one of the objects from the bowl, carry the object across the room, and place it in the empty bowl.

5) Have your child continue until all the objects have been moved to the bowl across the room.

6) Let your child follow the same procedure to bring each object back and place it in the first bowl.

KITCHEN GARDEN

In this natural science activity, vegetable tops sprout into a mini-garden.

1) Slice 1-inch tops off a carrot, a beet, and a turnip, making sure that any greenery has been removed first.

2) Let your child stand the vegetable tops in a shallow dish and add about 1/2 inch of water.

3) Have your child observe the cuttings over the next few days, adding more water as necessary.

4) In less than a week, your child should begin to see delicate, fern-like leaves growing from the carrot top, tiny green and red leaves sprouting from the beet top, and coarser, bright green leaves appearing from the turnip top.

5) Let your child continue to tend the Kitchen Garden as long as desired, watching also for threadlike roots to appear and spread in the water.

LI'L SPROUTS

Observing how seeds sprout is the focus of this natural science activity.

1) Place a sponge in a saucer and let your child add water until the sponge is wet.

2) Select three or four dried lentils or lima beans and let your child place them on top of the sponge. Explain that the beans are seeds from which bean plants grow.

3) Place the saucer where your child can easily observe the seeds, making sure that the sponge is kept wet at all times.

4) Within a week, your child should be able to observe the seeds swell, break through their skins, and sprout. Point out the two halves of each seed from which a sprout is growing.

ANOTHER IDEA: To continue the activity, let your child plant the sprouted seeds in a clear-plastic cup that has been filled with potting soil. Place the cup in a sunny spot and have your child add water when necessary.

FUN WITH MAGNETS

Use this activity to give your child practice in listening to and following directions.

1) Give your child five or six kitchen magnets and a non-aluminum baking sheet to use as a magnetboard.

2) Give directions for your child to follow such as those below.

   • "Put one magnet in the middle of the board and one magnet in each corner."

   • "Put one magnet on the board. Put another magnet above it and one below it."

   • "Put the yellow magnet at the top of the board, the red magnet in the middle, and the blue magnet at the bottom."

   • "Put two magnets on the board. Add one more. Count with me to see how many magnets there are now."

ORANGE LEMONADE

This color-mixing experiment is a tasty way to demonstrate how the color orange is made.

1) Have your child observe as you add red food coloring to water in a clear pitcher.

2) Pour the water into an ice cube tray and freeze.

3) With your child, make lemonade from scratch or from a mix.

4) When the ice cubes are partially frozen, pour a glass of lemonade for your child. Talk about the yellow color of the drink.

5) Give your child one of the red ice cubes to put in the glass and let him or her stir it with a spoon.

6) Discuss what happens to the color of the lemonade and why. (It turns orange because the red food coloring is being mixed with the yellow lemonade.)

7) Let your child help serve the remaining lemonade and ice cubes to family members or friends and explain how this color experiment works.

SQUISH BAG

This sensory-awareness activity provides hours of fun with no mess.

1) Make colored gelatin according to the package directions and allow it to set.

2) Place one resealable plastic bag inside another.

3) Fill the inside bag partway with gelatin, press out the remaining air, and seal the bag.

4) Press out the air in the outer plastic bag and seal it also.

5) Give the bag to your child to hold and "squish," encouraging him or her to tell you how the bag feels to the touch.

6) Store the Squish Bag in the refrigerator when not in use.

ANOTHER IDEA: Make several Squish Bags, each one containing a different material, such as flour, salt, uncooked rice, or dried beans. Ask your child to compare the various textures.

MAKING BUTTER

Your child will enjoy eating this science experiment.

1) Fill a small jar about halfway with whipping cream and screw on the lid.

2) Show the jar to your child and ask him or her to predict what will happen to the cream when you shake it.

3) Together, take turns shaking the jar and observing the cream as it thickens into whipped cream.

4) Continue shaking the jar, for a total of about 5 minutes, until butter forms.

5) Remove the butter and the liquid buttermilk from the jar and let your child compare them with some of the cream from which they were formed.

6) Rinse off the butter with cool water and add a little salt, if you wish.

7) Spread the butter on crackers or bread for tasting.

SNIFF, SNIFF

Exploring the sense of smell is the aim of this sensory-awareness activity.

1) In separate cups, place several different kinds of foods or spices with distinctive aromas, such as peanut butter, chocolate, a lemon half, an onion wedge, cinnamon, or cloves.

2) Have your child close his or her eyes.

3) Hold one of the cups up to your child's nose and ask him or her to describe the aroma. Is it sweet? Salty? Spicy? Can your child name the aroma?

4) Follow the same procedure with each cup.

5) Ask your child to tell you which aroma was his or her favorite.

AGE VARIATION: Let older children sniff bottles of different food flavorings, such as vanilla or peppermint, and try to name the scents.

FOIL FUN

This open-ended craft activity is sure to spark your child's imagination and provide hours of fun.

1) Give your child a roll of aluminum foil. Discard the box with its sharp cutting edge.

2) Sit with your child and tear off a piece of the foil.

3) Show your child how to tear, fold, mold, and pinch the foil to make such things as a magic wand, a ring, a bracelet, or a crown.

4) Also demonstrate how to use larger foil pieces with tape to make armor or a robot costume.

5) Encourage your child to use his or her imagination to create other objects with the foil.

6) When the activity is over, store the foil pieces in a box or bag for your child to play with again another time.

WHERE IS IT?

This predicting activity helps your child develop concentration.

1) Turn three paper cups upside down and arrange them in a row.

2) Place a small object, such as a dried pasta shape or dried bean, under one of the cups.

3) While your child watches, move the cups around within the row.

4) Ask your child to guess under which cup the object is hidden.

5) After the object is discovered, let your child hide it, move the cups around, and have you guess under which cup it is hidden.

EGG CARTON COUNTER

Math activities can be just as much fun with this homemade toy as with a store-bought one.

1) Use sharp scissors to punch a hole in the bottom of each cup in an empty egg carton.

2) Close the lid and turn the carton upside down so that the egg cups are facing up.

3) Set out twelve clothespins.

4) Let your child insert the clothespins into the holes in the egg cups, counting as he or she does so.

5) Remove some of the clothespins from the counter and have your child count how many are left.

6) Repeat, each time inserting clothespins or removing them and having your child count how many are left in the counter.

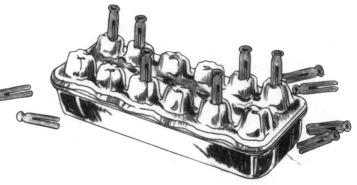

BEDROOM

SILLY TEDDY GETS DRESSED

This storytelling activity uses a teddy bear to help your child understand sequence.

1) Select a teddy bear.

2) Lay out doll or infant clothes that will fit the teddy bear, such as shoes, socks, pants, a shirt, and a hat.

3) Make up a story about Silly Teddy who puts on his clothes all wrong when he gets dressed.

4) Tell the story to your child, using the doll or infant clothes to demonstrate.

5) You might begin by saying that first Teddy puts on his shoes, then his socks. Next, he puts his pants on over his head and pulls his shirt up over his legs. Finally, he puts his hat on his hand.

6) At the end of the story, remove the doll clothes.

7) Let your child use the bear and the clothes to tell you a story about how Teddy dresses.

ALARM CLOCK FUN

Your child will have fun playing this simple listening game with an alarm clock.

1) Have your child stand outside the room.

2) Set a nonelectric alarm clock to go off in several minutes.

3) Hide the clock in a place that is accessible to your child.

4) Have your child come back into the room and begin to search for the clock.

5) When the alarm goes off, have your child use the sound as a clue for locating the clock.

LET'S PRETEND

Try doing this dramatic-play activity when you are changing the sheets.

1) Spread a sheet out on the floor.

2) With your child, imagine various things that the sheet might be.

3) For example, pretend that the sheet is a boat for you and your child to sail in. Or, imagine that it is a magic carpet and have your child tell what he or she can see as you take a make-believe ride on it.

4) Continue by pretending that the sheet is a pot of sticky glue, or a wide river.

5) Encourage your child to come up with other pretend ideas.

DRESS-UP BOX

Dressing up is a popular dramatic-play activity that promotes language development.

1) In a box, place old clothes and accessories for your child to play with.

2) Include such items as dresses, shirts, trousers, jackets, aprons, neckties, hats, scarves, shoes, gloves, eyeglasses (with lenses removed), and jewelry.

3) Place a mirror near the box for your child to look at while he or she dresses up.

4) Ask your child to tell you what he or she is pretending to be in the different dress-up outfits.

BUTTON BOX GAMES

Buttons are perfect items to use for sorting activities.

1) Set out a box of various kinds of buttons.

2) Give your child a drawer organizer or a similar kind of sorting tray, if available.

3) Sit with your child and encourage him or her to sort the buttons in different ways, such as by kind, color, shape, size, material, or number of holes.

4) Can your child think of other ways to sort the buttons?

SHOE FUN

Your child will practice matching skills with this pairing activity.

1) Collect four or five pairs of shoes.

2) Mix up the shoes and place them in a pile on the floor.

3) Set out four or five shoeboxes, if available.

4) Ask your child to sort through the shoes and find the pairs.

5) Have your child line up the pairs of shoes or place each pair in a separate shoebox.

ANOTHER IDEA: Follow the same procedure using pairs of gloves or mittens.

SMALL, MEDIUM, LARGE

This activity uses socks and shoes to help your child develop matching skills.

1) Collect one small, one medium, and one large pair of socks.

2) Mix up the socks and place them in a pile.

3) Ask your child to sort through the socks, find the pairs, and lay them out in a row on the floor.

4) Follow the same procedure using a small, a medium, and a large pair of shoes.

5) Have your child match the small pair of socks to the small pair of shoes, the medium pair of socks to the medium pair of shoes, and the large pair of socks to the large pair of shoes.

BEDSPREAD PEEKABOO

Try doing this predicting activity when you are making the bed.

1) Gather several familiar objects, such as a toy, a sock, a belt, a comb, and a necklace. Show the objects to your child and ask him or her to name each one.

2) Have your child stand with eyes closed as you fold back the bedspread and hide one of the objects under it, leaving a small part of the object exposed.

3) Let your child open his or her eyes and try to guess what the object under the bedspread is.

4) Follow the same procedure using the other objects.

5) Let your child hide objects under the bedspread and have you guess what they are.

ANOTHER IDEA: Use a blanket or sheet instead of a bedspread.

LAUNDRY TIME

Your child will help you organize the laundry with this sorting activity.

1) Before washing, set out laundry in a laundry basket.

2) Let your child help you sort the laundry by kind (sheets in one pile, towels in another pile, etc.) or by color (whites in one pile, colors in another pile).

3) After washing, let your child help sort the laundry by kind or by owner (Mom's clothes in one pile, Dad's clothes in another pile, etc.).

PILLOW FUN

You might wish to join your child in this whole-body movement activity.

1) Collect as many pillows as you can and pile them up in the middle of the floor.

2) Let your child jump barefoot into the pile of pillows.

3) Encourage your child to jump in a variety of ways, such as backward, on one foot, or sideways.

4) Spread out the pillows in a pathway and invite your child to jump from pillow to pillow.

5) Can your child imagine a magical place where the pillow path might lead?

BEAR BOUNCE

Children (and teddy bears!) love this movement activity that promotes large-muscle development.

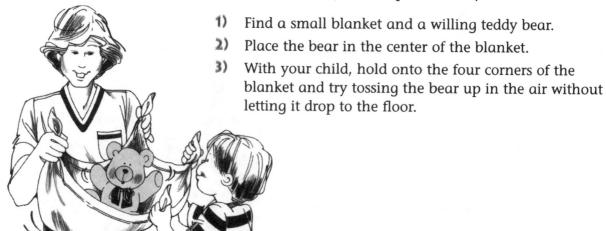

1) Find a small blanket and a willing teddy bear.

2) Place the bear in the center of the blanket.

3) With your child, hold onto the four corners of the blanket and try tossing the bear up in the air without letting it drop to the floor.

SOCK TOSS

This game is a great eye-hand coordination exercise.

1) Select several socks and roll each one up into a ball.

2) Place an empty laundry basket in the center of the room.

3) Have your child stand next to the laundry basket and drop the socks into it.

4) Gradually, have your child stand farther and farther away from the laundry basket and try to toss the socks inside.

5) When a comfortable distance is established, join your child and take turns tossing the socks into the laundry basket.

BUTTON UP

Have your child try this small-muscle development activity any time you are working in the bedroom.

1) Select a cardigan sweater (one with buttons down the front).

2) Drape the sweater over a chair back with the buttons facing out from the back of the chair.

3) Let your child stand behind the chair and practice buttoning from the bottom and working up.

HINT: It will be easier for your child to get the buttons in the proper button holes if you have him or her start buttoning from the bottom and work up.

STATIC ELECTRICITY

This science experiment works best on a cold, dry day.

1) Tear a small piece of tissue paper into bits.

2) Select a hard plastic comb.

3) Use a wool cloth, such as a scarf, a sock, or a fabric scrap, to rub back and forth over the comb several times.

4) Wave the comb over the tissue paper bits and have your child observe what happens. (The tissue pieces rise up and stick to the comb. This happens because rubbing the comb with wool charges the comb with static electricity, which "attracts" the tissue bits.)

5) Let your child rub the comb with the wool cloth and try picking up some of the paper pieces.

ANOTHER IDEA: Rub the comb with the wool cloth. Then hold the comb near your child's hair as he or she looks in a mirror. What happens? (The hair rises up to touch the comb.)

FABRIC PICTURES

This art activity provides a way to recycle fabric scraps.

1) Select fabric scraps that contain small pictures of such things as flowers, toys, or animals.

2) Cut out several of the pictures and give them to your child along with a piece of construction paper and some glue.

3) Let your child glue the fabric pictures on the paper any way he or she wishes.

4) Allow the glue to dry.

5) Have your child use crayons or felt tip markers to draw a large picture on the paper, incorporating the smaller fabric pictures.

AGE VARIATION: Older children may be able to cut out the fabric pictures themselves, using safe scissors.

MIRROR, MIRROR

Help your child learn to identify different body parts with this body-awareness activity.

1) Stand with your child in front of a full-length mirror.

2) Together, identify body parts, noting numbers of arms, legs, fingers, and toes.

3) Name different body parts such as head, ear, chest, elbow, and foot. As you do so, have your child point to those parts while looking into the mirror.

ANOTHER IDEA: Give your child a hand mirror. Ask questions such as these: "How many eyes do you have? What color are they? Can you stick out your tongue? Can you puff out your cheeks?"

SPECIAL ME

This self-esteem activity works well any time your child needs a special pat on the back.

1) Select a box with a lid.

2) On the bottom of the inside of the box, use strong glue to attach a small mirror.

3) Close the box and give it to your child.

4) Ask a question such as, "Who is the most special person in the world?" or, "Who did such a good job setting the table?"

5) Have your child open the box and look into the mirror to find the answer.

6) Repeat the activity as often as you wish.

ANOTHER IDEA: Let your child decorate the outside of the box with crayons or felt tip markers. Print your child's name on the lid.

BATHROOM

BATH MAT GAME

Use this listening activity to help your child learn how to follow directions.

1) Spread out a bath mat on the floor.

2) Start by giving your child one direction at a time, such as: "Sit on the bath mat. Put one elbow on the bath mat. Roll on the bath mat."

3) Continue by giving two directions at a time, such as: "Put one foot on the bath mat and then two feet. Put a washcloth on the bath mat and then a bar of soap. Fold the bath mat and hang it on the side of the tub."

4) Make up other directions for your child to follow.

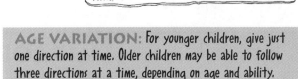

AGE VARIATION: For younger children, give just one direction at time. Older children may be able to follow three directions at a time, depending on age and ability.

HAND LOTION LETTERS

This letter-recognition activity also helps soften hands!

1) Find an unbreakable hand mirror.

2) Spread a layer of hand lotion over the mirror glass.

3) Using your finger, draw an alphabet letter, such as the first letter of your child's name, in the hand lotion.

4) Let your child use his or her index finger to trace over the letter while saying its name.

5) Smooth out the hand lotion to "erase," and start again by drawing another letter for your child to trace.

6) When your child has mastered a letter, take turns drawing and tracing it.

7) At the end of the activity, clean off the mirror with soap and water.

BATHTIME BUBBLES

Try doing this creative-play activity while bathing your child.

1) Select an empty thread spool and remove the papers that cover both ends.

2) Show your child how to dip one end of the spool into water and rub it on a wet bar of soap.

3) Then demonstrate how to blow through the other end of the spool to create rainbow-colored bubbles.

4) Let your child continue to dip the end of the spool into water and rub it on the soap bar before blowing each set of bubbles.

5) Keep the spool bubble blower with your child's other bath toys, if you wish.

SHAVING CREAM FUN

Your child is sure to enjoy using shaving cream for this open-ended art activity.

1) Set out a colored plastic tub, such as a dishpan or an infant bathtub.

2) Spray a puff or two of unscented shaving cream into the tub.

3) Let your child use his or her fingers and hands to smooth out the shaving cream and create designs in it.

4) Show your child how to "erase" by smoothing out the shaving cream whenever he or she wants to make new designs.

5) When the activity is over, just rinse your child's hands and the tub with water for a quick, easy cleanup.

MIRROR DRAWINGS

This art activity proves that drawing does not always have to be done on paper.

1) Give your child a damp bar of soap.

2) Let your child use the soap bar to draw pictures or designs on a mirror any way he or she wishes.

3) At cleanup time, just wipe the mirror with a damp cloth.

ANOTHER IDEA: For a more structured activity, have your child try using the soap bar to outline on the mirror the reflection of his or her face or other object.

BATHROOM MATCH

Look through bathroom drawers to find small items to use for this matching activity.

1) Collect two each of small bathroom items such as barrettes, hair rollers, combs, emery boards, small soaps, or cotton balls.

2) Place one of each item in a separate section of a sorting tray, such as a plastic drawer organizer.

3) Put the remaining items in a basket or box and mix them up.

4) Let your child remove the items from the basket, one at a time, and place them in the sections of the sorting tray that hold matching items.

ANOTHER IDEA:
Place all the items in the basket, mix them up, and let your child sort through them to find the matching pairs.

HOW MANY POUNDS?

Your child will enjoy learning how to use your bathroom scale with this math activity.

1) Set out a bathroom scale.

2) Fill a large plastic bottle with water, screw on the cap, and place it on the scale.

3) Show your child how to read the scale to discover how much the bottle weighs.

4) Help your child weigh himself or herself on the scale. Hand your child the bottle of water and let him or her discover what happens.

5) Have your child help you weigh yourself.

6) Try standing on the scale with your child. Figure out how much you weigh together.

GOOD HYGIENE GAME

This memory activity provides an opportunity to discuss good hygiene with your child.

1) Collect bathroom items that are used for good hygiene, such as a comb, a hairbrush, a bar of soap, a washcloth, a toothbrush, and a tube of toothpaste.

2) Set out several of the items.

3) Have your child examine the items and name each one.

4) Ask your child to close his or her eyes while you remove one of the items.

5) Let your child open his or her eyes and guess which item is missing.

6) Follow the same procedure with the remaining items.

AGE VARIATION: Use fewer items for younger children. Include more items for older children and change their position each time you repeat the activity.

Brighter Vision Publications

COTTON SWAB STRUCTURES

This activity is great for encouraging eye-hand coordination as well as small-muscle development.

1) Set out cotton swabs.

2) On a flat surface, arrange four swabs in a square so that the ends of the swabs overlap.

3) Show your child how to add four more swabs, one at a time, on top of the first four.

4) With your child, keep adding four swabs at a time to the structure as long as you wish.

5) Take the structure apart.

6) Encourage your child to reuse the cotton swabs to make more structures.

SINK OR FLOAT?

This simple science experiment encourages the process of discovery.

1) Collect several objects that sink, such as a washcloth, a nailbrush, and a full bottle of shampoo, and several objects that float, such as a sponge, a rubber duck, and a bar of Ivory Soap.

2) Place the objects in a basket or box.

3) Fill the sink or a plastic tub with water.

4) Give your child the basket of objects.

5) Have your child drop the objects, one at a time, into the water to discover if they are sinkers or floaters.

6) Together, look around the room to find other appropriate objects your child can use for this experiment.

EVAPORATION

This science activity helps your child become more aware of what happens in his or her environment.

1) Let your child hang up two or three wet washcloths and observe how they dry.

2) Ask your child to speculate about what happened to the water that was in the washcloths.

3) Explain that the water evaporated. It became vapor and escaped into the air.

4) To demonstrate that the water is still in the air, fill a large jar with ice cubes and screw on the lid.

5) Put the jar in a warm place where your child can observe the little drops of water that appear on the outside of the jar.

ANOTHER IDEA: Use the condensation that forms on a bathroom mirror or window after a hot shower to demonstrate that water is in the air all around us.

RACING TALCUM POWDER

This experiment demonstrates a bit of science "magic."

1) Fill the sink or a shallow plastic tub with water.

2) Let your child help sprinkle talcum powder, or any kind of body powder, on the water's surface.

3) Add a drop of liquid soap to the water.

4) Have your child observe as the powder "races" to the sides of the sink. (This happens because the soap breaks the surface tension of the water and pushes the powder to the sides of the sink as it spreads.)

5) Repeat the activity as often as you wish, changing the water and removing any traces of soap each time.

FAMILY FOOTPRINTS

Your whole family can participate in this growth-awareness activity.

1) After bathing your child, place a piece of thin paper on the floor beside the bathtub.

2) Help your child step out of the tub and place a wet foot on the paper to make a footprint.

3) Allow the paper to dry.

4) Ask each member of the family to follow the same procedure after taking a bath or shower.

5) With your child, examine the different crinkly footprints on the sheets of paper, talking about how the smaller prints belong to the younger family members and the larger prints to the older members.

6) Let your child arrange the footprints from smallest to largest or from largest to smallest.

HINT: To make the footprints stand out more, lightly trace around them with a pencil while they are still wet.

BATHING BABY

Help your child learn the names of different body parts with this body-awareness activity.

1) Put your child into the tub for his or her bath.

2) Give your child a plastic baby doll and a small washcloth or sponge to play with.

3) Start bathing your child, naming different body parts, such as arms, back, fingers, and toes, as you wash them.

4) Have your child copy you by washing the same body parts of the baby doll with the washcloth or sponge.

COTTON BALL COUNT

Cotton balls are perfect to use for this math activity.

1) Give your child a small container such as a toothpaste box, a paper drinking cup, or a plastic soap box.

2) Let your child stuff the container as full as possible with cotton balls.

3) As your child empties the container, count with him or her the number of cotton balls that were inside.

4) Give your child a different container and start the activity again.

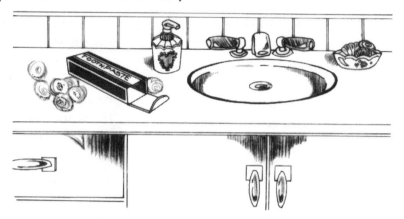

BANDAGE FUN

Your child will love using bandages for this body-awareness activity.

1) Give your child some adhesive bandages.

2) Show your child how to open one of the packages and get the bandage ready to put on.

3) Ask your child to place the bandage on a particular body part such as an arm or a knee.

4) Or, ask your child to put the bandage on you and then name that body part.

5) Repeat the process until all the bandages have been used.

ANOTHER IDEA: Dab cologne or bath splash on parts of your child's body as he or she tells you where to apply it.

CONSERVING WATER

Conserving water will become meaningful to your child when doing this science activity.

1) Find two large plastic bowls, preferably the same size.

2) Put one bowl into the sink and have your child wash his or her hands with the water running into the bowl.

3) When your child has finished, turn off the faucets, remove the bowl of water, and set it aside.

4) Put the second bowl into the sink and wash your hands, turning off the running water whenever it is not needed.

5) Remove your bowl from the sink and put it next to your child's bowl.

6) With your child, compare the amounts of water in the two bowls. Have your child tell you which way of washing hands used the most water and which used the least.

7) Let your child experiment with washing his or her hands the way that saves the most water.

BATHTUB POURING FUN

This activity teaches both eye-hand coordination and math skills.

1) While you are bathing your child, put a set of plastic measuring cups into the bathtub.

2) Let your child play with the cups, filling them up with water and pouring the water out.

3) Encourage your child to pour water from the smaller cups into the large cup. How many half cups does it take to make one cup? How many quarter cups?

4) End the activity by pouring water from one of the measuring cups down your child's back and letting him or her try to guess which one was used.

BATHTUB SQUEEZING FUN

Encouraging small-muscle development is the aim of this squeezing activity.

1) While you are giving your child a bath, put a clean sponge into the water.

2) Encourage your child to pick up the wet sponge and try to squeeze the water out of it.

3) Give your child a wet washcloth to squeeze, demonstrating how to twist the cloth to get the water out.

4) Provide your child with several clean plastic squeeze bottles, such as those used for shampoo or liquid soap, to play with in the water.

ANOTHER IDEA: Let your child try squeezing water into small containers such as plastic cups or bottles.

NOSIE ROSIE PUPPET

Turn a bathroom paper cup into a puppet for a fun oral-language activity.

1) Select a small paper drinking cup to use for making a Nosie Rosie Puppet.

2) Using sharp scissors, poke a hole in the side of the cup large enough for a child's finger to pass through.

3) Above the hole, poke two smaller eye holes.

4) Show your child how to put his or her hand up into the cup and stick a finger out through the large hole to make a wiggly "nose" for Nosie Rosie.

5) Encourage your child to manipulate the puppet while telling stories or singing songs.

GARAGE

RECYCLING STATION

This sorting activity teaches your child about helping to care for the environment.

1) Collect three cardboard cartons.

2) Using a felt tip marker, label the first carton "Newspapers," the second carton "Cans," and the third carton "Glass."

3) Place the boxes in a row in an accessible place to make a Recycling Station.

4) Help your child put a few discarded newspapers, cans, and glass jars or bottles into the appropriate cartons.

5) Encourage your child to use the recycling cartons on a regular basis.

6) When the cartons are full, let your child help take the contents to a local recycling center.

ANOTHER IDEA: Add more cartons as needed, depending on how items are recycled in your area.

ROPE LETTERS

Using whole-body movements makes this letter-recognition activity special.

1) Select a long piece of rope.

2) Use the rope to form an alphabet letter, such as C, on the floor.

3) Name the letter and talk about it with your child.

4) Have your child start at the top of the rope letter and walk along the rope in the direction that the letter is written.

5) Then let your child hop, skip, or jump around the outside of the letter.

6) Continue by forming other rope letters such as I, J, L, O, S, V, W, and Z.

CARPENTRY CREATION

This open-ended art activity provides practice in working with wood.

1) Collect small wood blocks and scraps.

2) Give your child sandpaper of different grades.

3) Let your child experiment with sanding the wood pieces, encouraging him or her to tell how the wood changes as it is sanded.

4) Set out a flat piece of board or plywood and some glue.

5) Let your child glue the sanded wood pieces to the board or plywood any way he or she wishes.

CARTON CONSTRUCTION

Encourage your child to use his or her imagination with this construction activity.

1) Collect several different sizes of cardboard cartons.

2) Give the cartons to your child.

3) Let your child arrange and stack the cartons in various ways to make different constructions, such as a house, a train, or a spaceship. Have your child tell you which construction he or she likes best.

4) When your child decides on a final construction, help him or her secure the boxes with tape or twine.

5) Place the finished construction where your child can play inside it.

ANOTHER IDEA: Let your child decorate his or her construction with crayon or felt tip marker designs or by gluing on paper shapes.

HARDWARE SORT

Your child will enjoy helping you organize your workbench with this sorting activity.

1) In a bucket, collect loose hardware items, such as nails, screws, hinges, and hooks.

2) Set out storage containers, such as plastic jars or margarine tubs.

3) With your child, place one of each hardware item in a separate container.

4) Help your child choose other items from the bucket and sort them into the containers that hold the same kinds of items.

SIZING UP TOOLS

Your child will enjoy using tools to do this ordering activity.

1) Select different sizes of a single type of tool, such as several sizes of screwdrivers or wrenches.

2) Give the tools to your child.

3) Let your child line up the tools from largest to smallest or from smallest to largest.

AGE VARIATION: With older children, talk about the kinds of jobs for which you would use the different sizes of tools.

ROUGH AND SMOOTH

Use this vocabulary-building activity to reinforce understanding of opposites.

1) Give your child a piece of sandpaper and a bottle of white glue.

2) Let your child squeeze the glue onto the sandpaper to make designs.

3) Allow the glue to dry.

4) Have your child run his or her fingers over the designs to feel the difference between the rough sandpaper and the smooth glue.

5) Together, name other things that are rough (a pine cone, a hairbrush, cement) and smooth (glass, paper, a slide).

TOOL GAME

Use tools to make a board game for this matching activity.

1) Collect several tools such as a hammer, a wrench, a pair of pliers, and a screwdriver.

2) Lay the tools on a large piece of cardboard and trace around each one with a felt tip marker.

3) Set out the piece of cardboard and the tools.

4) To play the game, have your child place the tools on top of the matching tracings.

FLASHLIGHT HOP

Your and your child will have fun with this whole-body movement activity.

1) Clear out a wide area in which to move around.

2) Dim the lights and turn on a flashlight.

3) "Hop" the beam of the flashlight across the floor and let your child run and jump onto it as it moves.

4) Let your child "hop" the flashlight beam on the floor for you to follow.

POUND AND COUNT

This eye-hand coordination activity involves using math skills.

1) Collect nails with large, flat heads.

2) Using a hammer, pound one of the nails partway into a piece of wood.

3) Give the hammer to your child.

4) Stand beside your child and let him or her finish pounding the nail into the wood while you count the number of strokes together.

5) Repeat the process as many times as you wish, using a new nail each time.

AGE VARIATION: Let older children try to guess how many hammer strokes it will take to pound in a nail. Help them compare their predictions with actual numbers of strokes.

NUTS AND BOLTS

This activity reinforces small-muscle development as well as matching skills.

1) Set out three containers, such as boxes or small plastic tubs.

2) Place several large nuts of various sizes in one container and matching bolts in another.

3) Show your child how to screw together one nut and one bolt.

4) Help your child match the remaining nuts and bolts and screw them together.

5) Have your child place the matched pairs of nuts and bolts in the third container.

WALKING THE LADDER

Try this activity for developing large-muscle coordination.

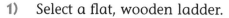

1) Select a flat, wooden ladder.

2) Lay the ladder on the floor.

3) Let your child start at the bottom of the ladder and walk "up" it, placing his or her feet on the floor between the rungs.

4) Have your child walk "down" the ladder in the same way.

5) Let your child try walking up and down the ladder with one foot on each edge. (Provide support as needed.)

BASKET SHOOT

This "basketball" game helps develop eye-hand coordination.

1) For a basket, set out an empty container, such as a trash can, a box, or a plastic bin.

2) Give your child several sheets of newspaper.

3) Let your child crumple each newspaper sheet into a ball.

4) Have your child "shoot" by tossing the newspaper balls into the basket.

5) Together, make more newspaper balls and take turns shooting baskets.

LIGHTING THE BULB

Try this easy science activity to spark interest in how electricity works.

1) Measure and cut out a 1-by-6-inch piece of aluminum foil.

2) Tear off a 6-inch piece of transparent tape and place it down the middle of the dull side of the aluminum foil to add sturdiness.

3) Fold the foil in thirds lengthwise, shiny-side out.

4) Tape one end of the foil strip to the flat end of a D-size battery and stand the battery on a table.

5) Help your child hold a flashlight bulb upright on top of the battery and touch the loose end of the foil strip to the bulb's metal side.

6) Together, observe as the flashlight bulb lights up. (Electricity flows from one end of the battery, through the foil, to the bulb and the other end of the battery. If any part of this circuit is missing, the light will not come on.)